Crystal Healing

Healing crystals, the human energy field, and how you can heal with crystals and gemstones!

Table Of Contents

Introduction	1
Free Bonus	2
Chapter 1: How Do Crystals Work?	3
Chapter 2: Wearing And Carrying Crystals Properly	5
Chapter 3: Using Crystals For Healing	8
Chapter 4: The Human Energy Field	12
Chapter 5: Crystals and Gems Commonly Used For Healing	15
Chapter 6: Choosing The Right Crystals For Yourself	20
Chapter 7: The Difference Between Crystals & Gemstones	23
Chapter 8: How To Clean & Recharge Your Crystals	25
Chapter 9: The Toxic Crystals To Avoid	29
Chapter 10: How To Use Crystals Alongside Psychic Healing	34
Chapter 11: The Different Chakras & How Chakras and Crystals Work Together	36
Chapter 12: Things You Can Heal With Crystals	40
Conclusion	44

Introduction

I want to thank you and congratulate you for taking the time to check out this book! This is the official edition 2 of this book, recently updated with additional information to make this book more complete!

This book contains helpful information about crystal healing, what it is, and how it works!

You will soon learn how to use crystals and gemstones for a variety of healing purposes, including headaches, pains, sore joints, lethargy, and more!

You will also discover the different ways that crystals can be used, and when you should use each method.

A detailed list of the different crystals and their benefits is also provided. With this list you'll be able to easily choose a suitable match for the particular ailment you're trying to heal.

This book will explain to you tips and techniques that will allow you to successfully understand and begin using crystals and gemstones to improve your life today!

You will also learn about how crystals work alongside chakras, how crystals can be used with psychic healing, the toxic crystals that you absolutely must avoid, and much more.

So, read on and begin harnessing the incredible healing powers that crystal have to offer!

Thanks again for picking up this book. I hope you enjoy it!

Free Bonus

As a thank you for taking the time to download my book, I'd like to offer you a **FREE** bonus!

I have compiled a list of my '7 Keys For Successful Meditation', and have made it free for you to download.

You can CLICK HERE to claim your free copy, or click on the link below:
http://bit.ly/1F91lfl

Meditation helps you to clear and focus your mind, and allows you to gain better control over your thoughts and focus. Regular meditation can make it a lot easier to successfully engage in things like Reiki healing, aura viewing, and opening your third eye, as these all involve deep and powerful use of your mind and focus.

So download my free report today – CLICK HERE – and begin experiencing the amazing benefits of meditation today!

Chapter 1:
How Do Crystals Work?

More often than not, people tend to think that crystals are just adornments for both the body and the house. However, this is most certainly not the case. There is a long tradition of crystals being used as a means of healing, not just the body, but the mind as well. Each crystal comes with a unique internal structure and this also causes a difference in the frequency at which it resonates.

Why is this frequency important? Well, it is said to be the very thing that provides these crystals the ability to heal. To heal with crystals, you need to understand how to apply these crystal frequencies properly in order to help restore balance and stability to the body's energy systems as well as stimulate its natural healing mechanism.

The great thing about using crystals as a therapeutic tool is that it is very gentle and also non-invasive. With crystals, you don't need to worry about damaging other body parts and internal organs while trying to heal. It is considered to be a form of alternative healing that works holistically, capable of harmonizing the mind, body, the emotions and spirit.

All of that, when combined, helps in increasing our overall feeling of well-being and helps in reducing the amount of negativity we carry with us. This is certainly great news, especially for those among us who might be going through bouts of depression or simply feeling overwhelmed by the weight of daily life.

There are many different ways that you can use crystals for this purpose. It basically comes down to personal preference but if you want a clearer idea, here are a few of the more common methods:

- Worn on the body as an accessory. Bracelets, rings and as a pendant for necklaces. It can also be worn close to the body; as a key ring or carried around in the pocket.

- Kept under pillows. This should allow the person to absorb the energy during sleep, when the body is most vulnerable.

- Used whenever bathing.

- Used during meditation.

- Placed around the house or in the work place.

- Creating gem essences.

- During massages, laying the stones on the body can help when it comes to Chakra clearing. They can also add another dimension to the massage itself.

- In the car, as a dashboard piece or hanging behind the mirror. Do remember that many of these gems offer protection so having it around while you're driving to and fro is certainly handy.

Regardless of how you choose to carry your crystals around, what matters most is knowing how to use them properly. Having this knowledge will enable you to maximize their full potential, and reap the benefits of crystals for yourself as well as for those around you.

Chapter 2:
Wearing And Carrying Crystals Properly

A simple place to begin with using crystals, is with the appropriate way of wearing and carrying them around. Most people who don't have any real knowledge of using crystals for healing would simply slap it on themselves and then hope that it works. This, of course, is not the way to go. As we've stated early on, the only way you can benefit from crystal healing is by using it properly. So to help you get started, here's a closer look at some of the methods mentioned in the previous chapter.

Wearing The Crystals

Now, crystals that are worn close to the body will have a more profound effect on the energy field coursing through it. The place where you wear it isn't critical if you're not targeting a particular area, but if you are, then you must be conscious of where you're wearing it. This is because of the fact that placing the stone over or near the area that requires healing helps it perform more efficiently, giving it a more focused effect. In some cases, it can also speed up the healing process because the energy goes directly to the spot where it is most needed.

You can also direct the crystal's energy to any area on your body through pure intention. There are instances, especially if you're quite intuitive, where you'll feel that the stone needs to be near a particular area. However it may be impractical to keep a crystal in certain places. For this, smaller pieces of crystal may be used and then placed into small pouches which you can pin inside your clothing for a more specific placement.

If you plan on wearing it as necklace, do make note of the fact that the length of your chain also has an effect on your crystal.

If your pendant is resting over the throat chakra, it would have an effect on the areas governed by it. At the same time, it would still provide energy to the other areas, though not of the same amount nor will it be as profound. So do keep this in mind if you intend on having the stone hanging around your neck. The more fine-tuned you are, the better the results will be.

Crystals In The Bath

It might be a new concept for a lot of people, especially for those who are using crystals as a means of healing for the first time. It is exactly what you think it might be, basically having the crystals in the bathwater with you or around the tub if you're not too keen on the former. This method is known to be very effective and gives your bath time a much needed boost.

What the crystal does is cleanse not just your physical body but cleanses all 4 levels of your being as well. It can help in removing any strains and stresses that you might have brought home from work or from simply being out in the chaotic world. If you've been harboring any negative emotions and have been feeling run down lately, this bath will help refresh you mentally as well as soothe, energize and revitalize you thoroughly. This is because the crystals absorb all of that negative energy and get rid of it for you. From there, its healing energies will be passed on to you and be directed to where they might be needed in your body. Some of the best crystals to use in this manner would be: aventurine, clear quartz, amethyst and rose quartz.

Creating Crystal Essences

A crystal essence is basically a liquid form of a particular crystal's energy pattern. These are typically made with simple water made more potent by the energy imbued in it. Water itself is a healing medium so when combined with crystals, it becomes even better. The great thing about crystal essences is that they can be used in more versatile ways when compared to the actual crystal itself. It can be used as an external treatment for anything that ails you and in some cases, even taken orally as a drink. Do note, however, that certain crystals may contain properties that are not safe for this so doing your research is key. To be safe, stick to the quartz family.

How to make crystal essence:

- Place your chosen crystal in a clean bowl filled with spring water. Leave it in overnight or if you can't, make sure that it soaks for at least 10 hours. Make sure sunlight reaches the bowl as well. The resulting liquid is your "mother essence".

- Once done, take a clear storage bottle and fill this halfway with brandy (which would act as a preservative) then fill the other half with your crystal essence. This is what's referred to as your stock bottle.

exposing it to sunlight helps with activating the memory energy of the water.

Chapter 3:
Using Crystals For Healing

Now that you know what you need to do in order to benefit from crystal healing, it's time you learned more about the different ways it can help. From providing you with relief physically and helping increase your zen mentally, here are the top ways through which crystals can aid us with everyday life.

Headaches

Typically, a person would just reach for the nearest bottle of Advil to help with this problem. However, this isn't always great for the body, and in the long run it can actually do more damage than good. Now, crystals which are non-invasive and very gentle can help you with it. The kind used would depend upon the type of headache you're having.

For example, tension headaches can be relieved by placing amber, amethyst or turquoise crystals on your head or around it. Migraines can be treated with lapis lazuli; this particular crystal has been in use for centuries when it comes to this purpose. Another common cause for headaches would be the imbalance between the solar plexus chakra and the head energy. This can be brought on by constantly eating unsuitable food or by stress. If you think that this is what you have or if you've been having headaches that come with an upset stomach, then you will need either a moonstone or citrine. Place this over the target areas and relax.

Insomnia

Much like treating headaches, the kind of crystal you'll need for this purpose will also depend on the cause of your insomnia. Some experimentation might be needed.

Now, if you think that your lack of sleep comes from over-worrying and anxiety, using sleep crystals such as amethyst, rose quartz, chrysoprase and citrine would help with this. Just place them near your bed or even under your pillow to help sooth your worries.

If your sleeplessness is caused by overeating then moonstone or iron pyrite can help your stomach calm down and allow you to sleep better. There are also instances where a person's insomnia is caused by constant nightmares. For this, protective stones such as smoky quartz or tourmaline can help out. They should be placed at the foot of the bed- some labradorite can also help as these crystals are known to ward off any unwelcome thoughts or feelings.

Lethargy/Lack of Energy

This is something that a lot of people tend to experience on a daily basis. Stress, overdue work, the chaos of simply living in a fast-paced city-- all of these things can certainly weigh a person down. However, don't fret! There are many crystals that can provide you with a boost to your energy level. To begin with, yellow, orange and red crystals are known to help with this. The most dynamic and energy stimulating varieties are those which have bright coloring. Golden-yellow topaz, golden amber and red garnet are great examples of this.

For motivation, use crystals with deeper tones such as dark citrine, tiger's eye and jasper. The way you hold a crystal can also factor into the effect it has on your entire system. For example, holding a clear quartz pointing upwards in each of your hands while placing a citrine over your solar plexus helps you achieve an instant increase in your energy levels that affects your whole body. So if you're feeling lifeless during the mornings, give this exercise a try and get off to a good start to your day.

Difficulty Focusing and Lack of Concentration

Often associated with stress and anxiety, difficulty concentrating is also a common problem in today's world-- due to many different factors. To help with this problem, you can make use of quartz which is well-known to aid in mental clarity as well as carnelian which helps in clearing out extraneous thought.

Other crystals that are great for this purpose are amber and citrine, both known to stimulate memory. Lapis lazuli is a very powerful thought amplifier, and amethyst can help you focus on the more realistic goals that you have and enable you to visualize things clearly. It is also capable of soothing your nervous system which benefits neural transmission as well.

For studying, some fluorite would be an excellent aid as it is known to balance out the functions of the brain hemispheres. Sodalite helps in communication, and enables you to better understand ideas and concepts involved in your studies.

Healing the Mind

You may not think much of it but the mind needs a break every now and then to recover from everything that it goes through every single day. Crystals are known to promote tranquility and peace of mind by eliminating any blockages that prevent proper emotional expression. These are the stones that should be worn or kept close to your body at all times. They can also be used for meditation.

When it comes to choosing crystals, there are plenty of options available. Start with green colored ones for this is a healing color and many crystals of this hue are known to help reduce nervous and mental stress. In eastern cultures, green jade is highly valued for its ability to help the mind relax and regain focus. Blue lace agate and rose quartz are both great for detoxifying and cleansing the emotions. Opal can be used to help promote emotional stability and balance.

Another great crystal would be amethyst, which helps in tempering hormone production which should aid in balancing a person's emotional highs and lows. This should also help get rid of that "scattered" feeling, allowing you to feel more in control. Another great benefit that amethyst can provide you with would be aiding in better focusing your energies and reducing any mental burdens that you might have. If you're experiencing a negative state of mind that you can't seem to shake off, amber can help in neutralizing this.

Chapter 4:
The Human Energy Field

We've discussed the human energy field quite a few times in relation to the healing power of crystals but what exactly is it? Also known as the "aura", this is a field of energy the envelopes and penetrates through the human body. It supports and underlies our bodily functions, and when blocked or hindered, causes these functions to go a little haywire as well. Contained within the aura are energy aspects of every function and structure of the body, along with everything that we have ever experienced, including: thoughts, physical sensations, feelings, states of consciousness and so on.

Energy tends to flow through this energy field via fine channels, otherwise known as nadis, which are also composed of energy. Where these nadis cross paths, energy centers or chakras are created. As they are major hubs when it comes to the distribution of energy, the chakras help in directing its flow, which then replenishes all of the glands, nerves and eventually, the entire structure of the body. Models created that mimic this energy field show layers of energy bodies within its structure.

It is through this energy field that we are able to connect with everything and everyone that exists. There are studies which have been able to measure this, as a matter of fact. However, crystal healing deals with energies that are far subtler and are therefore, not detectable by scientific instruments.

How do we know that the energy field actually exists?

If it can't be measured scientifically then how do we know that it actually exists? Well, our knowledge of the human energy field mostly comes from collected ancient texts as well as metaphysical literature. There are some people who can also observe the aura through what's referred to as a high sense perception otherwise known as clairvoyance, the ability to see what can't be reached by the average physical sight.

Besides clairvoyance, there are also a few other ways through which the aura can be perceived. There are also people who are sensitive to the energy field but are able to hear it instead of seeing. Some can even experience it in the form of taste and smell. In most cases, knowledge of the energy field can also be had through a sense of intuition or knowingness-- once you become more familiar with it.

Human energy field models and why they are needed:

Those who are able to observe the aura have also attempted to describe it by using different models, all of which show its structure as they perceive it to be. However, this is quite tricky as not everyone can see the aura in the same way. This is one of foremost reasons as to why there are a number of different models available. All have the same value but none can singularly describe what the aura is like. Models that are 3D are actually quite limited in their capacity to fully show the subtlety and complexity of what they are attempting to describe.

It is also important to note that these are no more than models and much like certain particles that don't have a defined structure or boundary, the subtle energy bodies have no such form either. Instead, they are perceived to be patterns of energy which can be both fluid and dynamic depending on many different factors. In fact, the subtler an energy is, the less localized it is and as such, the more difficult it becomes for any person to describe or represent it in a three dimensional manner.

Do healers need to create their own models?

If you are looking to really further your healing knowledge or if you're trying to develop your ability to sense energy, among the things you need to remember would be staying open to what can be experienced besides the ones shown in existing models. Some healers work with models which are unique to them and work best for their style of healing. Creating your own model also has its value when you're attempting to communicate something with your client with regards to the nature of the healing you're doing. The more familiar you are with it, the better you'll be able to explain as well as perform.

Chapter 5:
Crystals and Gems Commonly Used For Healing

Blue Kyanite

One of the most common sources of pain as well as disability would be back pain. Blue Kyanite is one of the best crystals for this purpose. It can help with different muscular problems and aids in bringing everything back into proper alignment. It is a potent pain reliever and can also provide healing benefits to other parts of the body such as the throat, thyroid and the urogenital system. It is also capable of lowering blood pressure, healing infections as well as getting rid of any excess weight.

Malachite

Feeling as if you're surrounded by burdensome negativity that's beginning to drain your energy away? Fret not because this protection stone can help you clear away all of that. It is one of the most powerful and is also capable of absorbing and guarding you from all kinds of radiation. This crystal is capable of treating swollen joints, fractures, arthritis and asthma, as well as stimulating the liver so it releases and gets rid of toxins. So if you need detoxifying within your body and mind, this would be the right crystal for your purpose.

Orange Calcite

Orange calcite is great if you've been experiencing blockage when it comes to your creativity. It can help in getting all your creative juices flowing and alleviates any feelings of depression at the same time. Because it is highly energizing, it makes for the perfect artist's crystal. Any chronic fatigue, mental breakdown and emotional fears that a person may have can be diminished just by simply having this around. Because of its warm energy, it is also calming and soothing, helping with restoring emotional balance in a person.

Citrine

This particular stone carries with it the energy of the sun. A stone of abundance, it will teach you how to attract prosperity and wealth among other good things. How does it do it? By helping increase your confidence and happiness levels, it also enhances your personal power. Ever heard of the saying that positivity attracts good? The same concept applies here. Not only that, if you're more confident and motivated about what you're doing, you also tend to become more productive hence the lifestyle improvement. For the body, it can help you prevent and reverse the effects of degenerative diseases. It also detoxifies and fortifies your nerves, helping you feel more energetic and ready for action.

Amethyst

Considered to be one of the most powerful protection crystals, the amethyst gives off a high level of spiritual vibration which can help safeguard you from any form of psychic attack. It is also one of the most effective tranquilizers and is capable of inducing higher states of consciousness. It can alleviate feelings of anxiety, fear, anger and even sadness. For those who want to develop their psychic abilities, it enhances intuition and aids those who are seeking spiritual wisdom. In terms of health, the crystal can help relieve stress and headaches as well as tension.

Chrysocolla

When it comes to treating arthritic pain as well as bone disease, Chrysocolla would be one of the best options available. It helps in relieving pain caused by arthritis, strengthens the thyroid and soothes burns. Typically referred to as the musician's stone, it helps improve a person's ability to communicate while promoting a tranquil and peaceful energy which draws out any negativity within and outside of the person using it. Also known as the stone of harmony, it alleviates guilt and amplifies truth.

Rose Quartz

Looking to attract love in your life or perhaps, a need to heal heartache? If this is the case then this particularly beautiful crystal is just right for you. A favorite among women because of its pink coloring, this powerful stone can bring about peaceful, loving and calming energy. It helps in healing and purifying the heart. It also brings forth inner peace and promotes unconditional love. Health-wise, it helps with treating different skin disorders while improving the skin tone and reducing wrinkles. Some say that it also helps with increasing fertility in women.

Carnelian

This helps in stimulating love and joy within us as well as clearing away any negative energy. It allows for light to enter our energy fields and begin the process of transformation. Kept at home, it can have a stabilizing effect on the energies within it and promote a sense of calm and harmony. It is also capable of awakening inner talents and unblocking creativity.

Coral

This aids imagination, and intuition, as well as further strengthens one's understanding of mysticism. It can also help alleviate any feelings of sadness or depression and is able to promote feelings of peace, quieting the restless mind. It will also help a person strengthen their connection to the universe's harmonious energies.

Garnet

This helps in revitalizing, energizing and balancing energies - quite perfect for the weary mind and tired body. It also inspires devotion as well as love, and enhances sexual energy. Often referred to as the stone of health, it is also capable of clearing away any negative energy while enhancing a person's personal power to attract more success and happiness in their lives.

Hematite

As a stone of mental mastery, it tackles many different aspects of our mind. It helps with enhancing memory, focus and concentration while deflecting negativity. It also stimulates a person's desire for inner happiness and peace while promoting their ability to love. This particular stone is also often used as a protection charm, kept in cars or in people's purses as it can dispel psychic attacks as well as negative outside influence.

Jade

Typically associated with love and virtue, it helps balance energies between partners as well as self - which allows for the person to feel in harmony with themselves as well as the people they are in relationships with. Often referred to as a fidelity stone, it is also often used to help relax both mind and body as it gives off a calming and soothing energy which allows for people to focus better and make wiser decisions.

Lapis Lazuli

The stone of protection and enlightenment, this particular piece aids with spiritual growth, objectivity and intuitive perception. It is mentally calming and can help whenever a person needs clarity. It can be of great use to students who might need a little help when it comes to organizing their daily activities without it leading to feelings of anxiety and stress. Another thing that this stone is great at would be promoting serenity and feelings of acceptance. Lastly, if you want better dreams at night then keeping this under your pillow will certainly help.

Moonstone

Typically referred to as the stone of changes as well as wishes, it helps in clearing any hindrances or obstacles that might be in the path of a person's destiny. It also enhances one's awareness of their own body rhythm, allowing the individual to gain better balance of their own natural energy. It also supports their overall well-being and can be used as a protection charm whenever needed.

Peridot

The stone of renewal and rebirth, it helps increase happiness and peace in a person's daily life. It also attracts good luck and success while efficiently protecting an individual against nightmares as well as negative energy. For people going through a break-up or any form of damaged relationship, this will help them to heal. Lastly, it promotes comfort and vitality when kept at home or close to the person- such as in their offices or car.

Chapter 6:
Choosing The Right Crystals For Yourself

Most people who want to use crystals for healing tend to have a particular purpose in mind. While certain varieties of crystals tend to yield the needed results, not all specimens contain the same properties (metaphysical or physical) even if they are from the same "family". It is for this reason that selecting the right crystal for your need is imperative. To help you get started, here's a simple and easy to follow process for choosing the right crystals and gems for healing.

- Be clear about your purpose. The more specific you are about it, the better your chances are of finding a good crystal match. Keep in mind that many of these crystals are multipurpose but also have specialty problems that they're best known for treating.

- Once you have a list of your requirements, you can begin searching. This should make the process much easier since you can easily narrow down the scope of the search itself. Through this, you can even filter out the ones with the most potential for healing so you increase your chances of finding the best one for your purpose.

- Lastly, pick the crystal that matches your vibrational frequency. This is actually the most important part of the process itself. By finding one that matches, you're able to amplify the benefits even more and make the healing much more potent. So, how is this done? First, you would need to hold the crystal you've chosen in your hand and keep your purpose in mind while doing so. Make sure that you state your purpose in an affirmative sentence, for this will allow for better energy flow. Focus on this and just let it take over. What you're looking for is a positive feeling coming from the crystal you're holding. Instinct will let you know if you have the right one in hand.

Increasing Your Inner Vibrational Frequency:

Whenever you're seeking the aid of a crystal, you're basically using it to increase your vibrational frequency as well. This is regardless of whatever use you have for it, the desired effect will always be this increase. This is why it's important for people to find a crystal that they match with when it comes to these frequencies. Not only will it make you feel good, it will also make the healing process quicker and more powerful.

Another thing to keep in mind would be the proximity of the crystal to the affected area or to your body. This constantly affects your own frequency so choosing the right one would actually boost it daily. However, choosing one that isn't a good match can actually negatively affect your vibrational frequency, causing it to lower and eventually get drained. You'll feel this physically as well. Lethargy and lack of motivation are just a few of the symptoms.

Quick Facts About Gemstones and Crystals:

- Each stone is usually made up of crystals which are always in motion and emitting a certain energy frequency.

- Humans can be affected by the weather, their surroundings, the food they consume or even the color they've chosen to wear. The same applies to gems and crystals.

- The energy field of these healing stones is also influenced by their geometrical form as well as their color and subtle vibrations. This is something to keep in mind when you're choosing one for yourself.

- Related to the above, color plays a pretty dynamic role when it comes to a stone's ability to heal and release energy. Colors can influence whether a particular stone is calming or stimulating, purifying or healing and so on. You can use a stone's color to further enhance its healing benefits and properties.

Chapter 7:
The Difference Between Crystals & Gemstones

Those who believe and practice alternative healing would usually use the terms "gemstones" and "crystals" interchangeably. Practitioners believe that these minerals emit certain vibrations that can help a person by subtly affecting their inner self and then bringing out the best in them. Both gemstones and crystals are also known for their healing powers and for attracting good karma. There are also crystals and gemstones that block negative energy and can combat bad vibes and other negative elements. Gemstones and crystals may seem similar to some, but they do have some very distinct differences that could surprise those who do not fully understand them.

Gemstones are precious or semi-precious stones that are made up of minerals. For a long time, gemstones were believed to be a source of great power and have been part of various legends and myths. Many considered gemstones as sacred treasures that may have amazing healing powers. Some people also believed that gemstones improved the user's inner abilities.

These days, gemstones are still considered to be precious treasures, but mostly because people use them as adornments in accessories and jewelries. They are polished, shaped and faceted to make into to jewelry and to add value. Some gemstones are very hard to procure, and artisans will need to use specialized tools to polish and refine them even further. This is also the reason why jewelries and accessories adorned with gemstones are expensive and very rare. Gemstones have 3 characteristics that give them their distinct qualities: durability, rarity, and overall attractiveness.

Crystals, on the other hand, are made from a pure and solid substance that follows a repeating and orderly arrangement of molecules and atoms within the three spatial dimensions. Not all crystals are precious or contain healing powers. Examples of these crystals are salt and frozen ice.

Crystals used for healing and other therapeutic purposes are more or less in the same league as gemstones in this regard. They come from bedrocks and are far more precious. A very good example of a precious crystal is a diamond. Crystals under this category emit energy that amplifies whatever it is you are feeling, thinking or wishing at a particular moment. For example, it is said that rose quartz crystals increase a person's chances of finding love when worn or placed inside his or her bedroom.

Both crystals and gemstones have different effects on your body and your inner self. Some people believe that wearing them could add protection from illnesses, bodily harm and negative elements. Others believe that they help you attract good karma and good fortune. Both crystals and gemstones are useful, and although it's commonly referred to as 'crystal healing', we will be using gemstones also.

Chapter 8:
How To Clean & Recharge Your Crystals

To get the most out of your crystals you must clean and recharge them. To clean crystals means cleaning them physically and then cleaning them of unwanted energies and vibrations that came with them before they reached you. Once you have cleaned your crystals you can recharge them for use later on.

It's always a good idea to clean your crystals the moment you receive them. This will ensure that your crystals are free from dirt and negative energies. The first part of cleansing your crystal entails physical cleaning. Crystals sometimes come with a few specks of dirt and mud. These are physical evidence of their origin. If you have mud or dirt on your crystal, simply use a soft cleaning brush to sweep off any dried up dirt and mud. A soft bristled toothbrush works well if you have no soft brush on hand. Brush off the dirt gently as the crystal can be brittle and might break off with hard brushing.

For more stubborn dirt and mud, you may immerse your crystal in lukewarm water and gently use the brush to clean them off. You can also use cool running water to clean your crystals. Do not use any harsh detergents or chemical cleaning agents to remove dirt off your crystals, as these can be potentially harmful. Some cleaning agents react with the components of the crystals that could either discolor them, or make them brittle.

Once you have physically cleaned your crystal the next step is to cleanse the negative energies that the crystal might have come in contact with before it got to you. This could include energies from the people who mined, handled, packed and transported the crystals; you do not need nor want these negative vibrations. In some cases, when other people decide to touch and handle your crystals it also transfers negative energy to them.

To cleanse your crystals of negative energies and unwanted vibrations you can soak them in a saltwater bath. Simply pour water taken from natural sources like spring water or from the sea into a basin. The water level should be able to cover the crystals completely by at least 1 inch. Soak the crystals for 24-48 hours. Make sure that you do not touch the salt water used to cleanse the crystal when you throw it away as you might transfer negative energy to yourself. Rinse the crystal carefully to get rid of the residue from the salt water bath.

Another cleansing method is to bury them in soil or sand. When the crystals are buried in the Earth they are "retuned" and revert themselves back to their original vibrations. Most people use a pot of soil or sand to bury their crystal so that they can easily remember where it was buried. This is also handy for when it's raining or snowing outside as some crystals are not hard enough to withstand rain and excess moisture. You can also bury them in wider spaces like your garden or backyard, provided you mark the place where your buried them so that they won't be lost. If your crystal has a lot of little nooks where dirt can get trapped, it might be best to do a salt bath rather than burying it in soil or sand.

Cleaning your crystals does not have to be a regular, daily or weekly task. Some people believe that you should cleanse it only when you feel like it is not performing the way it should. The frequency of cleaning your crystals will depend on how often you use them and for what purpose. Some crystals used for healing and other rituals need to be cleaned afterward while others don't. In the end, it usually depends on how you feel about your crystals when you use them.

After performing a physical cleanse and a cleansing of negative energies and vibrations, your crystal is now ready for recharging.

When you use a crystal for a healing or cleansing ritual, you take up its positive energies and transfer them to yourself. Even if you just wear them simply for personal use, they can absorb negative vibes and energies thus depleting their positive energy. That is why you need to recharge and revitalize your crystals. Here are some common methods to recharge crystals.

1. Sunlight – Sunlight is a great source of positive energy and power for crystals. Sunlight is especially great for quartz crystals. A sunbath can make quartz crystals look brighter and make its colors look more vibrant. Place crystal near the window for at least 1 hour for smaller, personal crystals and longer for bigger, more elaborate crystals. Do not place them under direct sunlight as this can cause the crystals' colors to fade.

2. Moonlight – The best time to recharge your crystals is during the full moon. The energies from the full moon are at their strongest and this effectively recharges and re-energizes your crystal. After recharging them under the full moon, they will feel more potent the next time that you use them. If you miss the full moon, do not fret. You can still recharge your crystals 2-3 days after the full moon. Leave the crystals in a place where they are in full view of the full moon and leave them to soak up the moonlight for as long as possible.

3. A Quartz Cluster – Place your crystal on top of a quartz cluster for at least 24 hours to energize and revitalize them. If you are afraid of scratching your crystal, you can put it in a pouch made of natural materials like cotton or silk.

4. Crystal Layout – Arrange other crystals in a circle and place the uncharged crystal in the middle. This allows them to channel different energies taken from different directions directly into the crystal in the middle. Use this method together with the sunlight or moonlight.

Chapter 9:
The Toxic Crystals To Avoid

While most crystals can heal the body and the soul, some are toxic to humans. You must never use these crystals to create elixirs and essences, or combine with essential oils to make massage oils. You need to handle these crystals carefully and you should not let them come in direct contact with any part of the body. When handling toxic crystals, you must always wear protective gear like goggles, masks and gloves.

Before going through the list of toxic crystals here are some safety reminders for handling them.

1. Wash your hands thoroughly after handling any stone. Even if the stone is familiar or if you already know its contents, wash your hands anyway. The crystal could still harbor toxic substances without your knowledge.

2. Consult a geologist or a mineralogist before handling a particular crystal. Some toxic crystals could look similar to non-toxic ones and could easily be mistaken as a crystal that's safe to handle. If you are unsure about the kind of crystal that you have, ask a geologist or a mineralogist to have a look.

3. If you suspect that you have been exposed to a toxic crystal, consult a health professional immediately. Some toxicity emitted by the crystals can be very harmful to your health.

4. Wear protective gear when handling crystals. Can't hurt you to wear gloves, or goggles when handling toxic crystals. Some toxic elements in the crystals can cause a rash when they come in contact with your skin.

5. Avoid handling them altogether if you can. Do not heat, alter them chemically, or combine them with other substances unless you have to. Some people do experiment on these crystals to find out more about them but they do it in a controlled and safe environment. They use safety measures to ensure that they handle these crystals with utmost care so never try to do this on your own or mix them together with essential oils, elixirs, and gem waters.

The most common toxic elements found in crystals that are harmful to human health when ingested are those that contain arsenic, aluminum, barium, cadmium, copper, lead, mercury, zinc and other toxic elements. Doctors and other health care professionals have warned people repeatedly to avoid these substances and stop using products that contain them. Lead, for example, is no longer used for making cosmetics and paint as it's harmful to human life. Mercury is another toxic substance that can be found in some crystals. Other toxic substances found in some crystals manifest themselves even though the substance wasn't ingested or inhaled. Some crystals also have radioactive elements contained within them so be aware of these things too.

The list below should help you know which crystals have toxic elements. Some of these you must avoid, and others you simply need to be careful with. The list may not contain names of all the crystals that you are using so if you are unsure then consult a professional if you're using an obscure crystal.

Actinolite - asbestos

Adamite - arsenic, copper and zinc

Ajoite - aluminum and copper

Alexandrite - aluminum

Altaite - lead
Amazonite - copper
Amblygonite - aluminum
Andalusite - aluminum
Antimonite - lead
Atacamite - copper
Aquamarine - aluminum
Auricalcite - zinc and copper
Azurite - copper
Barite - barium, lead and zinc
Beryl - aluminum
Black Tourmaline - aluminum
Boji-stones - sulfur, pyrite
Brazilianite - aluminum
Bronchantite - copper
Cavansite - copper
Celestite - strontium
Chalcantite - copper
Chalcopyrite - copper and sulfur
Chrysocolla - copper
Cinnabar - high levels of mercury
Conicalcite - copper
Copper - extremely poisonous
Covellite - copper and sulfur
Cuprite - copper
Dioptase - copper
Dumortierite - aluminum

Emerald - aluminum
Fluorite - fluorine
Garnet - aluminum
Gem Silica - copper
Galena - lead
Garnierite - nickel
Iolite - aluminum
Kunzite - aluminum
Labradorite - aluminum
Lapis Lazuli - pyrite
Lepidolite - aluminum
Malachite - copper
Markasite - sulfur
Mohawkite - copper and Arsenic
Moldavite - aluminum oxide
Moonstone - aluminum
Morganite - aluminum
Pietersite - asbestos
Prehnite - aluminum
Psiomelan - barium
Pyrite - sulfur
Realgar - sulfur and arsenic
Ruby - aluminum
Sapphire - aluminum
Serpentine - asbestos
Smithsonite - copper
Sodalite - aluminum

Spinel - aluminum
Spodumene - aluminum
Staurolite - aluminum
Stibnite - lead and antimony
Stilbite - aluminum
Sugilite - aluminum
Sulfur - Poisonous
Sunstone - aluminum
Tanzanite - aluminum
Tiger Eye - asbestos
Topaz - aluminum
Tourmaline - aluminum
Tremolite - asbestos
Turquoise - copper and aluminum
Vanadinite - vanadium
Variscite - aluminum
Vesuvianite - aluminum
Wavellite - aluminum
Wulfenite - lead and molybdenum
Zircon - zirconium, radioactive
Zoisite - aluminum

Chapter 10:
How To Use Crystals Alongside Psychic Healing

One of the most prevalent uses for crystals has a lot to do with psychic healing. As earlier mentioned, crystals emit different vibrations that could help restore balance to one's inner self. The same vibrations are also known to aid in the healing process when the crystals are used properly.

Psychic healing is also known as spiritual healing. To be healed spiritually the person must accept and believe unconsciously that they will be healed in order for the psychic healing to work its powers. If the person does not believe in their mind that they will be healed, the process of spiritual healing may not work as well as expected or not at all.

To use crystals in conjunction with psychic healing, the healer must first know the properties and vibrations that each crystal emits. They must know what the effects of the crystals could have on the person and must use them accordingly. Some healers are not used to using crystals when they heal people but when they do, they amplify and hasten the healing process and could sometimes yield better results than when not using crystals. With the right use of crystals, you can restore your balance and attain a healthier body, mind and spirit.

Once the healer has determined the right crystals to use in order to heal the person, they should be able to harness the energy and vibration from the crystal and channel it to the proper areas in the body, mind and soul in order for it to work properly. You should channel the powers of the crystals on the areas of the body that have certain chakras. Each chakra corresponds to a part of the body, so focusing on that chakra can help to heal the body. With proper channeling of the energies of the crystals to the right chakras, the healer can target the correct areas that will be most effective in the healing process.

Another great way to use crystals in psychic healing is by wearing them as accessories. If you're not fond of wearing crystals or any type of jewelry, just keeping them in your pocket can prove to be beneficial. Some crystals do not just heal; they also protect you from harm. Tiger eye for example can be used for protection and grounding. You can increase their healing powers and hasten the healing process by placing these crystals in certain places in your home.

Psychic healing not only affects the body but also the mind and spirit. The crystals also affect the body, mind and soul in ways that no medicine will ever do. Psychic healing can sometimes be attributed to a change in disposition and a more positive outlook about life and can immensely help a person physically and emotionally. Combining this type of healing with crystals only increases the benefits.

Chapter 11:
The Different Chakras & How Chakras and Crystals Work Together

The term "chakra" comes from the Sanskrit word that means "wheel". Clairvoyants see chakras as revolving, colorful spheres surrounding the body. The strength of each chakra varies from one person to another. This can be evidenced by which colors of the chakra dominate your entire aura.

There are 7 chakras major known to man but many psychics believe there are more chakras that are yet to be discovered and unlocked. Each chakra corresponds to the colors of the rainbow. The chakras start at the base of the spine and end on top of the head. Each chakra vibrates and responds to different speeds. If a particular chakra is blocked, the body becomes imbalanced and so it develops illnesses. Blocked chakras can also be the cause of emotional and physical problems that people encounter on a day to day basis. Crystals have certain vibrations that when directed to the blocked chakra can help make the energy flow once again and heal the body and mind.

The first major chakra is the Muladhara, or root, and it aptly rests at the base of the spine or the tailbone at the back of your body, and in the pubic bone on the front. This chakra is where the most basic needs of men like the need for security and survival lies. In the physical sense, it governs sexuality, especially in men. It is also attributed to stability and man's intrinsic need to protect his own life. The color attributed to the root chakra is red and the symbol used for this chakra is a lotus bearing four petals. When this chakra is blocked, the person tends to feel anxious, insecure and fearful. Blockage can cause problems with expressing sensuality, problems in the sexual organs, and eating disorders. Use crystals like garnet and black tourmaline to clear the blockages and let the energy flow back from the chakra.

The second major chakra is the Svadhishthana, or the sacral. It is located in the sacrum, the area that is roughly 2 inches below the navel. This is where the sexual energies of women come from. The sacral is symbolized by a crescent moon encased within a white lotus that has six orange petals. Naturally, the color associated with this chakra is orange. The sacral chakra governs areas of reproduction, sense of self-worth and ability to relate to others both sexually and personally. Physical problems that occur when this chakra is blocked include constipation and kidney problems. Tiger eye, orange calcite and carnelian agate are the crystals that can help open up this chakra.

The third major chakra is called the Manipura or the solar-plexus. It resides below the breastbone and is usually related to the digestive system. The symbol used for the solar plexus is an inverted triangle with 10 yellow petals surrounding it. The color associated with this chakra is yellow. The solar-plexus is the source of personal power and can be attributed to one's passion and impulses. It is the source of man's ego, anger and strength. When this chakra is out of balance the physical problems that can occur include digestion problems, food allergies, liver problems and diabetes. Emotional problems that can occur when this chakra is blocked include depression and lack of self-confidence. Return the balance of this chakra with yellow calcite, topaz or citrine.

The fourth chakra is the Anahata, or the heart chakra. You can find this chakra just behind the breastbone and in between the shoulder blades. The heart chakra obviously governs the heart, love and compassion. It is also the center of spirituality. The heart chakra is symbolized by a circular flower with 12 petals encasing a hexagram. This can sometimes be interpreted as two intersecting triangles facing opposite direction that symbolize the union between a man and a woman. The color attributed to the heart chakra is green and pink. When this chakra is blocked, you may experience feeling afraid of letting go (separation anxiety) and getting hurt and feeling unworthy of love. It also affects how you give and accept love from others. Physically, when this chakra is out of balance you may have a heart attack, insomnia, or high blood pressure. Rose quartz and kunzite can help strengthen this chakra and can help you to attract love.

The fifth chakra is the Vishuddha, or the throat chakra. It is symbolized by a silver crescent encased within a downward pointing triangle surrounded by 16 light blue petals. The colors associated with this chakra include pale blues and turquoise. Because it is located in the throat area, it naturally corresponds to a person's way of communicating with people and self-expression and creativity. Timidity is an effect of an imbalanced throat chakra and it may make you unable to express your thoughts clearly as well. Physical problems relating to ears and throat happen when this chakra is out of balance. Aquamarine and azurite both help increase the powers within this chakra.

The sixth chakra is the Ajna, or the third-eye chakra. You can find this chakra right above the eyebrows in the center of the forehead. It is symbolized by a lotus that has only two petals with a triangle in the middle making it look like an opened eye. The color associated with this chakra is deep blue or indigo. Practitioners attribute higher intuition, gut feelings and psychic powers to this chakra. The ability to make decisions, wisdom and imagination also resides in this chakra. When out of balance, the problems you may encounter include headaches and blindness. Emotionally, you may feel less assertive and indecisive. Lapiz lazuli, amethysts and sodalite are the gems that help restore balance to this chakra.

The last major charka is the Sahasrara, otherwise known as the crown chakra. The crown chakra is located at the top of the skull. It is symbolized by a lotus with a thousand petals of different colors. The main colors attributed to this chakra are white and purple. It is the center of enlightenment, consciousness and dynamic energy and thoughts. It is the key that holds the connection between man, and divine beings and God. Practitioners believe that the soul enters and exits the body at the top of the head and through this chakra. An unbalanced crown chakra leads to unhappiness, destructive feelings and frustration. Physically you may get migraines, headaches and other problems relating to the head. Emotionally you will feel depressed and unable to connect and believe in a higher power. Amethysts, Oregon opals and clear crystal quartz all relate to this chakra in a positive way.

Crystals play a major role in unblocking and returning balance to any of these chakras. Rituals involving the laying of these crystals in the area of the chakra that is blocked and unbalanced can help restore the chakra back to its opened state. Setting up crystals associated with this chakra inside your room or personal area can also greatly enhance their healing power and open you up to a more positive and healthy outlook in life. They can also act as protection from any harm that may ruin the balance of your chakras.

Evaluate yourself, your personality and emotions, and then determine which chakras may be blocked. Start by focusing on healing the lower chakras first, and as their problems alleviate you can continue moving upward, allowing the energy to flow until you reach your crown chakra!

Chapter 12:
Things You Can Heal With Crystals

You should understand by now the powerful effects of crystals to the human body and mind. It was mentioned earlier that crystals have their own vibrations and natural energies that are also contained within the human body. When these vibrations and natural energy comes in contact with the body, it transfers these energies to the body. It also restores the body's equilibrium and cleanses the mind and spirit. It provides positive vibes and can sooth away any negative energy that's blocking the chakras in your body.

Some crystals can heal one or two problem areas in your body while other more powerful crystals provide you with a holistic healing that extends to your entire physical, mental, emotional and spiritual needs. No single crystal can heal every ailment you have, so healers usually combine and arrange several types of crystals together to address your body's problem areas during the healing process.

The different parts of the body can benefit from several crystals all at once. Some people wear a combination of several different crystals around their neck and wrists or conceal them somewhere else. People who do this believe that the presence and proximity of these crystals help protect them from harm and continuously heal them as they go about their daily lives.

Each crystal can target a certain part of the body and can be used to improve health and well-being. Crystals tap into the body, mind and spirit in order to heal the person of whatever it is that's been ailing them. Here are some great examples of the things that crystals can do for the body, mind and spirit.

1. Improves concentration – if you've ever felt like you cannot focus on doing something or if your thoughts feel scattered and cluttered, then you can use tiger eye, amethysts or calcites to help you gain focus. Though technically this is not an ailment, many people suffer from this problem because of the multitude of distractions around them.

2. Returning your appetite for sex – for couples who are experiencing sexual problems, orange crystals like the carnelian can greatly influence the reproductive organs and helps overcome frigidity, increases sexual drive and fertility, and relaxes sexual anxieties.

3. Restores vitality – citrine, clear quartz and green tourmaline all help bring positive energy into your life. Green tourmaline raises your energy, helps you sleep better and is considered an all-around healer. Clear quartz is known to be beneficial to healing both the mind and body and restores the body's energy after it is depleted.

4. Depression – depression can be caused by a number of things, some of which can be attributed to an imbalance of the chakras. It is a debilitating emotional problem that can potentially push a person to their death when not dealt with properly or when ignored. A person suffering from depression should be surrounded by friends and family and a solid support system that they can count on. Crystals that help alleviate depression include smoky quartz, lepidolite and tiger's eye. These crystals absorb negative thoughts and energies around you making you feel lighter and less bogged down by problems.

5. A broken heart – time is said to be the best cure for a broken heart. But when time takes too long and you feel like you need to move on, you can count on crystals to help you get better. Crystals like pink lemurian seed and pink manganocalcite increase feelings of self-worth and soothe the soul after going through a lot of emotional trauma.

6. Stress relief – another thing that is technically not an illness but could be a cause for illness is stress. An increase in stress levels can cause heart problems, sleep disruptions and digestive problems so it is important to address stress before it affects your body. Crystals that help fight stress include turquoise, hematite and citrine. Use these crystals daily and also include a few minutes of meditation and relaxation to your day and you'll feel less stressed.

7. Aids in weight loss – many people suffer from obesity and eating disorders that make them gain weight. The excess weight causes a person to lose their sense of self and feel defeated and lonely. Iolite supports detoxification and helps reduce fatty deposits around the body while apatite can suppress hunger and raise your metabolic rate.

Using crystals to heal yourself can be very beneficial to your entire being. Consult a healer if you can in order to be properly guided with the abilities of each crystal and how they can help you heal. Healers also have great experience and more effective ways to help make you get better faster. The dangers of handling raw crystals also pose a threat to your physical well-being so if possible, let healers handle them first.

Your body, mind and spirit are all interconnected. When one is affected, the rest are hard pressed at functioning properly. Remember to enrich all three with crystals that enhance your abilities and see the difference it makes in your overall health. Remove negative thoughts and create a positive aura as much as you can. Negative thoughts can breed and fester and make you sick in the process so it's best to maintain a positive outlook as much as you can.

Most healers will say that a lot of your problem can be cured as long as you believe, acknowledge and accept that you can be cured. Whether you are looking to heal your body, mind or spirit, crystals are definitely great tools that can help you to feel better. The vibrations and energies contained in different crystals can target any ailment and health problem you might have and improve your emotional and physical well-being. Use these crystals together with other methods like meditation, prayer, proper diet, exercise, rest and relaxation. Open your heart to the healing properties of crystals and you might find the cure that you've been unable to find with conventional healing.

Conclusion

Thank you again for downloading this book!

I hope this book was able to help you learn more about Crystal healing!

The next step is to put this information to use, and begin using the power of crystals and gemstones!

Also don't forget to download my **FREE** report on the 7 Keys for Successful Meditation by following the link - http://bit.ly/1F91lfl

Finally, if you enjoyed this book, please take the time to share your thoughts and post a review on Amazon. It'd be greatly appreciated!

Thank you and good luck!

www.ingramcontent.com/pod-product-compliance
Lightning Source LLC
LaVergne TN
LVHW012103070526
838200LV00073BA/3408